I is for Inuksuk

An Arctic Celebration

Mary Wallace

MAPLE
TREE
PRESS

Maple Tree Press books are published by Owlkids Books Inc.
10 Lower Spadina Avenue, Suite 400, Toronto, Ontario M5V 2Z2
www.owlkids.com

Distributed in Canada by Raincoast Books
9050 Shaughnessy Street, Vancouver, British Columbia V6P 6E5

Distributed in the United States by Publishers Group West
1700 Fourth Street, Berkeley, California 94710

Acknowledgments

I would like to thank Ama Alariaq for her help in choosing the words for this book,
and Betty Brewster, manager of Inuktitut legal translation at the Department of Justice,
Nunavut, for her help with the translation. And a very special thank you to Sheba Meland
for all her ideas and inspiration.

Cataloguing in Publication Data
Wallace, Mary, 1950-
    I is for Inuksuk : an Arctic celebration / Mary Wallace.

ISBN 978-1-897349-57-1 (bound). – ISBN 978-1-897349-73-1 (pbk.)

    1. Inuksuit--Juvenile literature. 2. Inuit--Canada--
Juvenile literature. 3. Inuit--Canada--Pictorial works.
4. Inuit--Canada--Social life and customs--Juvenile
literature. I. Title.

E99.E7W344 2009   j305.897'12071   C2009-900998-6

Library of Congress Control Number: 2009923341

Design & Art Direction: Word & Image Design

Canada Council   Conseil des Arts
for the Arts   du Canada

ONTARIO ARTS COUNCIL
CONSEIL DES ARTS DE L'ONTARIO

We acknowledge the financial support of the Canada Council for the Arts, the Ontario Arts Council,
the Government of Canada through the Book Publishing Industry Development Program (BPIDP),
and the Government of Ontario through the Ontario Media Development Corporation's Book Initiative
for our publishing activities.

Printed in China

A   B   C   D   E   F

Life in the Arctic

For thousands of years, people living in the Arctic have built stone towers called Inuksuit* to guide them across this land of snow and ice. A single marker is called an Inuksuk. It can mark where to find food or how to get home. It can even be a way of saying "Welcome." Even though the Inuit no longer live as nomads, moving from place to place with the seasons, hunting caribou and seal, and living in igloos as their ancestors did, the Inuksuit remain as a symbol of the Arctic. Look for Inuksuit to guide you as you read through this book. Turn to page 32 to find out their meanings.

*See the Inuktitut pronunciation guide on page 32.

I is for Inuksuk

ᐃᓄᒃᓱᒃ

I is for Inuksuk,

the stone messenger that stands at the top of the world.

Stones are carefully chosen to fit together. A finished Inuksuk can stand up to fierce snowstorms.

For more than
4,000 years, Inuksuit
have guided Arctic
travellers.

Inuksuit show this hunter where to find fish to bring home to his family.

N is for Nanuq

�óᓄᖅ

N is for Nanuq,

the powerful polar bear of the North.

The polar bear is a good summer swimmer.

In winter she roams over sea ice, sniffing out seals' breathing holes.

Her huge paw is perfect for walking across thin sea ice.

She feeds her cubs and keeps them safe and warm in her den beneath the snow.

U is for Umiaq

ᐅᒥᐊᖅ

U is for Umiaq,

the family's summer sea boat.

As the boat passes, a huge bowhead whale splashes her fluke.

From the shore, a giant wrinkled walrus watches
the family go by.

In the deep, dark sea below the boat swim
schools of Arctic char.

K is for Kamik

ᑲᒥᒃ

K is for Kamik,

a warm waterproof boot made from seal and caribou skin.

A rounded ulu is used to cut the kamik from the hide.

Children learn to sew perfectly tight stitches to keep out the frosty Arctic air.

Pants and mittens are made from animal skins, too. Girls' amauti have large hoods. Parkas are for boys.

S is for Siku

ᑯᑦ

S is for Siku,

the Arctic sea ice that changes with the seasons.

Seals live on and below the thick winter ice.

When the weather starts to warm,
sea ice breaks up and floats away.

Without sea ice to
travel across, the fluffy
sled dog must wait on shore.

In spring and summer, the Inuk navigates his qajaq, or
kayak, made of skin and bone through the frigid sea.

U is for Umimmat

ᐅᒥᖕᒪᒃ

U is for Umimmat,

the shaggy muskoxen that share the tundra with other wildlife.

Each spring, herds of hungry caribou search the tundra for lichen to eat.

The snowy owl soars high above in the chilly air.

The coat of this Arctic hare changes from grey to white in winter.

Shy and small, an Arctic fox darts across the snowy tundra.

K is for Kunik

ᐊᓂᒍᖅ

K is for Kunik,

a soft kiss that says we're family.

The igloo keeps the family warm and cozy, away from the fierce winds that blow outside.

Everyone gathers round the soapstone qulliq. Its burning seal oil gives light and heat.

The rhythmic sounds of throat singers carry across the long winter night.

The drum dancer celebrates the joys of Arctic life.

Inuksuit and Their Meanings

Look for these Inuksuit in the illustrations throughout the book.

ᐃᓄᖕᒍᐊᖅ

Inunnguaq (ee-noon-wawk) means "image statue." It is built in the shape of a person.

ᓂᑭᓯᐃᑦᑐᖅ

Nikisuittuq (nee-kee-soo-eet-took) means "North Star." It points to the North Star in the winter sky.

ᓇᒃᑲᑕᐃᑦ

Nakkatait (nak-ka-ta-eet) means "things that fell in water." It points to a good place to fish.

ᖃᔭᒃᑯᕖᑦ

Qajakkuviit (ka-yak-vee-eet) means "kayak rests." It is a place to store a kayak while it dries.

ᐱᕈᔭᖃᕐᕕᒃ

Pirujaqarvik (pi-roo-ya-kar-veek) means "where the meat cache is." This stone marker shows where meat is stored.

ᑐᐸᔭᖃᖕᒐᐅᑦ

Tupjakangaut (toop-ya-kang-oot) means "footsteps of game." It steers hunters toward good places to find animals to hunt.

ᐃᓄᒃᓱᒃ ᖁᕕᐊᓱᒃᑐᖅ

Inuksuk Quviasuktuq (ee-nook-sook ku-vee-a-sook-took) means "Inuksuk expressing joy." It is an Inuksuk that is built to express the joy of the place and the builder.

Inuktitut Pronunciation Guide

Amauti	*a-ma-oo-tee*	Inuktitut	*ee-nook-tee-toot*	Qulliq	*ku-leek*
Inuit	*ee-noo-eet*	Kamik	*ka-meek*	Siku	*see-koo*
Inuk	*ee-nook*	Kunik	*koo-neek*	Ulu	*oo-loo*
Inuksuit	*ee-nook-soo-eet*	Nanuq	*na-nook*	Umiaq	*oo-mee-ak*
Inuksuk	*ee-nook-sook*	Qajaq	*ka-yak*	Umimmat	*oo-mee-mat*